Travels in the American West

Travels
in the
American West

Photographs by Len Jenshel

Smithsonian Institution Press, Washington and London
Published in association with Constance Sullivan Editions

This series was developed and produced for the Smithsonian Institution Press
by Constance Sullivan Editions

Editors:
Constance Sullivan
Susan Weiley

Smithsonian editor:
Amy Pastan

Designed by Katy Homans

The paper used in this publication meets the minimum requirements of the
American National Standard for Permanence of Paper for Printed Library Materials
Z39.48-1984.

First edition

Printed by Meridian Printing, East Greenwich, RI, USA

cover: *Dante's View,* Death Valley National Monument, California, 1990

The photographs were made in part with the support of the Graham Foundation for
Advanced Studies in the Fine Arts.

The photographer wishes to thank Chevrolet for providing assistance in making many of
the photographs possible.

All photographs reproduced in this book are courtesy of the Laurence Miller Gallery, New York City.

Why did you choose to photograph the American West?

It happened quite by accident or out of a series of developments. The only time in my life that I did not live in New York City was when I lived in Denver between the ages of nine and eleven. That was when I got my first taste of the Rockies. Then in 1980 I received a Guggenheim Fellowship and took a cross-country trip, which was an eye opener. I was seduced by the beauty and the space of the landscape. It was liberating to be out where you could see horizons, and sky and weather patterns. As the project progressed I went to the national parks and found myself doing things more and more in the way that a tourist would—flying out, renting a car, going to the scenic overlooks. My concerns began to center around the controversy of development within the park system. The contrast between the myth of the West and the magic of the landscape is one of the key elements for me.

Did you go there with predetermined ideas about how the landscape would look?

I had preconceptions, we all do, based on photographs, Western movies, television, and certainly there is the great American Western myth, but the other part is getting away from all of that and seeing the place for what it really is. Part of what photography does so well is to dispense with preconceived notions, reeducate, and reshape one's thinking and attitudes about places and things—even history.

Were you influenced by the great nineteenth-century photographers of the American West, like Carleton Watkins, William Henry Jackson, and Timothy O'Sullivan, who went out to record the way the landscape looked and how it was changing? Do you consider yourself a landscape photographer in that tradition?

Very much so. I'm extremely influenced and moved by those photographers' work. Part of my intrigue with their work is how surreal and mysterious these places often look in the pictures—like they had gone to the moon, and were sending pictures back home to show other people what it looked like.

When I'm out there working, I sometimes feel like an archaeologist. I want to do a similar thing in some fantasy-like way, which is to pretend I'm going to a place that no one has ever set foot on, and I am deciphering clues of

5

a past existence based on a tire track, or a cattle guard. The nineteenth-century photographers who were concerned with landscape often put people in their pictures to show scale, to show that the Sequoia tree or a shooting geyser was 250 feet tall. I do not include people in my landscapes, but I'll include the detritus or the evidence of a human race, almost like an archaeological dig.

Many of your photographs include traces of human influence, such as orange highway cones, or weather instruments, or roadside rest stops, while others invite the viewer into the frame—for example, through an open car door off to one side. Why not photograph just the landscape without that paraphernalia?

Because that's what's there, and it's what I see and am drawn to. I'm interested in how these places are being used. They were once natural and now they're more like museums or Disneyland. They've been developed for any number of reasons—for their beauty, or their interest, or their geology, and I try to show that aspect very subtly in these pictures.

I want to portray both the beauty and development, especially in the national parks, by showing first a beautiful landscape that seemingly resembles a picture postcard, then including some trace of human influence, such as a scenic overlook or a road.

Most people go to the national parks, drive their car to the vista point, get out and take a picture, or sometimes they snap from inside the car. That's what my photograph with the open car door is largely about. "The Mittens" in Monument Valley is an instant symbol of the myth of the Great American West. John Ford's westerns were filmed in front of these classic buttes. What I tried to convey was something of the perverse relationship between the grandeur and the machine. Cars and buildings are what we sometimes feel most at home with in wide open spaces, rather than the splendor or unique-ness of the landscape.

My work is about fitting in—fitting in with your environment. There is a definite humor in the harmony (and irony) of scenic-overlook walls mimicking the view. Then, of course, the car also mimics "The Mittens." And there's a whole other reference to a spoof of the advertising industry—the classic car-in-the-Southwest shot.

And did you ever stop and think why they call it "The Mittens"? The most unusual rock formations and geological wonders are named after familiar man-made architectural structures: "the Cathedral," "the White House," "the Courthouse," "the Chimneys." In the salt flats of Death Valley, "Devil's Golf Course" has more mystique and more draw for the average tourist than the scientific name for these strange salt formations. We rely on personification and metaphor to get a handle on what is most mysterious and unfathomable.

The Western landscape is vast and magnificent. How do you decide what to photograph, or when to stop and take a picture, in such an overwhelmingly beautiful and seductive setting?

I think it's instinctive. Anything is capable of stopping me. All the things that I think my pictures are about—awe, humor, irony, myth, metaphor—will challenge me in different ways when I'm working. I don't go out there looking for a preconceived picture. I walk, or hike, or drive in a car, and something happens that makes me stop, confront the scene, and take a picture. It could be beautiful light, or a great butte in the distance, or tire tracks, or a new building going up. For those of us who work intuitively, as opposed to conceptually, a very high premium is placed on instinct.

What are some of your other photographic concerns?

Light. Certainly the light out West is very special and very seductive. It's so different from Northeast light—it's crystal clear and has a language and a sensuality all its own. I think part of my loving the light out West has to do with the fact that this is such a romantic project—this fantastic landscape is bathed with the most beautiful light imaginable—well, maybe not, because sometimes I exaggerate it with my headlights.

Why?

To heighten the romance and myth and make it look even more theatrical—like a stage set. I think adding that theatricality and drama is wonderful and humorous—perhaps because it is so surreal to begin with—why not up the ante? Also, it brings the car into the picture, and a lot of these pictures are about traveling in an automobile. Driving at dawn and dusk, your headlights can't help but bask this cactus or that tree and it takes on a whole new dimension—becomes a whole other visual idea. It certainly is about the light and the automobile.

What about the picture-postcard aspect of your work? Are these photographs supposed to show people who've never seen the West what it looks like?

Yes, in a funny way. I remember when I was a student, Garry Winogrand said, in reference to the snapshot aesthetic, that he thought the most amazing photographs look like they could have been taken by a five-year-old, because of their naive, innocent, and spontaneous look. I think I've adapted that somehow into photographing landscape. To me that's what the picture post-card is all about. There's a presence and an immediacy to it that anyone could respond to. I don't know or care if my pictures will actually ever end up in one of those little postcard racks or ever bring people out to the West, but basically I want them to have that kind of feeling. It's really important to me that on some level the pictures are not heavy handed, but delicate, and subtle, and effortless.

Traditionally, the great landscape photographers who worked in the American West shot their pictures in black and white, but you use color. How does color differently describe the landscape than black and white?

When I began to use color in 1973, there was an interesting dilemma facing students of the fine arts. It seemed that if you wanted to work in a "straight" documentary style tradition, you used black and white. If you wanted to make a living, you used color. Period!! I want to say color is more "real," but I don't believe that's true because color is just as odd an abstraction as black and white is. Photography is such an abstraction of the thing photographed.

Color brings a whole new vocabulary to the photographic language. It's a very difficult question to answer—it's just a different ball game.

Do you think color is more convincing than black and white? When you look at a black-and-white photograph by Watkins or O'Sullivan or Ansel Adams, is it less persuasive?

Not really. That has more to do with how something is photographed by the artist than whether it's in black and white or color.

Your pictures have been described as lush, sumptuous, sensual, and picturesque. Can you talk a bit more about the way you relate to color film and use it in your work? How does it influence your thinking?

Using color has evolved and I find myself responding more and more to rich color harmonies now. You start to see the world differently as you learn more about the tools of your medium—about how they describe something. They begin to redefine the thing itself and certainly how you relate to it.

When I was studying with Winogrand in 1973, and we were first experimenting with color, he said that you can use "hot" colors but you have to tame them and that you are much better off avoiding them at all cost. So in the beginning I was challenged to use color monochromatically, to *not* be sensual with it. Over the years I have gradually rejected that thesis and have become much more atuned to the lushness, the beauty of color and colors. The first color assignment Winogrand gave us was to pretend we had black-and-white film in the camera, which was really astounding, the idea that maybe it's not about color at all—maybe it's about photography. Over the years I've spent much time contemplating this—and finally rejecting it. Color has its own language, which is different than black-and-white. It is going to bring out different elements like harmony, like chromaticism and very specific color relationships, and hence different meanings.

I see in color. I'm currently photographing volcanoes and geysers and geothermal areas with my wife, Diane Cook, who works in black and white. We work together on a lot of these trips and sometimes we'll take the same trail and I'll see something and say, "This doesn't work in color but I think it's a black-and-white picture," and she'll say, "This doesn't work, I think it's a color picture." To me this points out a lot of the differences between these two mediums when we're doing this collaboration. So the color is very much an issue and I embrace that. I want to be open to seeing everything that color can do in photography. Formally, color functions differently in every photograph.

What formal considerations are important to you? What has to be in a frame to make it a successful composition?

Again, it's impossible to generalize. Lately, however, I've been noticing an interesting pattern. I start with a very symmetrical frame. If there's an object—a cactus, a tree, a mountain—it often ends up right smack in the center of the picture. This relates to what I was saying about being a tourist or about the picture postcard, or how would a five-year-old frame the picture? For me, the photograph starts with the thing itself; like a red Joshua tree lit by the taillights of my car, or a glowing bush floating in the center of a sea of cobalt blue, or the tunnel in the mountain in Zion National Park. There is often a real symmetricality to my work. But that's only the beginning. Framing is critical for me, as well as graphics and tension.

I love what Robert Adams said in *Beauty and Photography* when he was talking about the photographic frame: "A tension so exact that it is peace."

How important is the editing process in your work? Do you shoot a lot?

I shoot quite a lot. One of the reasons I don't use a view camera is because I like the spontaneity of a medium-format camera (6 x 9 cm). This tool allows me to make more variations on a theme. The deliberateness of seeing with a view camera requires that you go to a place, walk around it two times or ten times, go back and forth, pick your spot, and take the picture from that spot. I'll see something I like, I stop, I take the picture immediately before the light changes or the adrenalin disappears. I don't want to lose that rush. Now, there might be a better picture three feet over to my left that I haven't seen yet, but I'll get to it eventually. I really like to shoot spontaneously and work out photographic ideas with many variations—then I edit the work later on.

Do your ideas about the way a place looks change when you see the prints?

It often changes completely. The photograph is so different from the thing photographed. John Szarkowski wrote that photography "shows us differently what we thought we knew."

You've been photographing this landscape for several years. How often do you go back?

I make about five trips a year of between one to three weeks each, sometimes to explore new places and sometimes to go back after I've familiarized myself with a place.

When I received the Graham Foundation Grant in 1988, I had two months to work and I covered almost the entire Southwest. But usually I cover less territory because I don't have that luxury of time.

Are your trips carefully planned or do they evolve while you're on the road?

Sometimes I stick to a plan—but I'm happiest when I'm spontaneous, like the 1988 trip. I was there in November, a time of year noted for the desert storms, so I completely rewrote the trip as I went along.

Is weather a major factor?

Absolutely. And so is atmosphere. Different weather patterns, like the storms in November, have dictated certain ideas that I've been working on. It would clear and snow and clear again within two hours. The skies were fantastic and that changes the landscape and the light as well as where you go and how you photograph it. It's wonderful when you can be open to different stimuli—as when you're in a place and you think you're taking one kind of picture, but the weather has a whole other idea, like when the landscape is covered with snow, or the sky lights up at dusk in that wonderful desert afterglow.

Another reason I decided to use the medium-format camera rather than the larger view camera is that although I'm very interested in detail, at one point atmosphere became equally important to me. That was the tradeoff—spontaneity for finer grain—and weather makes you most aware of those changes.

You photograph the clichés of the West—Zion National Park, Yellowstone National Park, Monument Valley. Are you sometimes intimidated by the familiarity of this subject matter? What do you hope to show us that we haven't seen before?

The challenge of the "cliché" is something that fascinated me the very first time I picked up color film. Transcending the cliché becomes the prime issue. Is there a way to make an intelligent photograph of a sunset after all the horrible things that calendar art and advertising photographs have done with that genre?

So the challenge is to go directly to the sunset or the national park and find out how to transcend the picture postcard. It is the ultimate challenge. When I fail, the photographs often look just like clichés, but when I've suc-ceeded—and upped the ante by incorporating that sensual, beautiful color of sunset or that late light, or a geyser in Yellowstone National Park—that makes the work even more exceptional and interesting. Metaphor makes the risk worthwhile.

Do you ever go back and rephotograph the same place?

It's actually an obsession of mine that Diane teases me about incessantly. She says, "You can't go home again." I insist you can, and I will probably spend my life returning to the scene of the crime.

How do you determine when you're finished with a particular series?

Any number of ways. At a certain point, while working on the Gilded Age mansion project in 1982, I began to notice that most of the good pictures had to do with sexuality. If you had told me that's what the project was about when I began, I would have said you were crazy. I was using photography like one who would interpret dreams. That was a fabulous discovery for me. I love how photography, when used intuitively, tells you about yourself and your relationship to the world. Anyway, once I was "on" to myself—and the hidden had become exposed—the work lost its charge, its vitality, its life. And that's how that particular project came to a screeching halt.

Does photographing the West have something to do with conquest?

Sure. When you say that, my association is to the volcanoes that I've been photographing in Hawaii, perhaps because of the power and conquest of nature. I might be trying to conquer these ideas and they're getting more and more strange and beautiful as I work on these projects, not unlike the landscapes themselves. Volcanoes and geysers are very volatile and explosive and dangerous. You're never the same once you've seen a live volcano and stand next to lava pouring into the ocean. It changes your life and you realize "I can't control that. I shouldn't even be this close, and what the hell am I doing here." But it's so mesmerizing, you're just kind of drawn to it the way a moth is drawn to a flame. So maybe conquering ends the project as well, for when you feel that conquest, it's no longer challenging or alive or crucial. The Western project doesn't feel close to being over. It feels like it could be a lifelong project.

**Is there a relationship between your photographs of
formal gardens and the Western landscape series?**

They're really the same. Control—control of nature—is central to both.
Gardens are planted to control your view at any given time of the year, control
your position through paths, etc. The National Park Service does the same
thing. Yes, I think they're exactly the same.

**Are your pictures always taken from the vantage
point of civilization, or do you sometimes go into the
wilderness to photograph?**

Both. The contrast is important. But the good pictures seem to come more and
more from within fifty feet of the car because I think I'm more connected right
now to those concerns. The project is really about the automobile's influence
on the landscape.

Joshua Tree National Monument, California, 1990

Dante's View, Death Valley National Monument, California, 1990

Zion National Park, Utah, 1988

Near Zion National Park, Springdale, Utah, 1988

Great Basin National Park, Nevada, 1987

Route 127 near Death Valley National Monument, California, 1990

Glass Mountain, Cathedral Valley, Capitol Reef National Park, Utah, 1987

Cathedral Valley, Capitol Reef National Park, Utah, 1987

Dante's View, Death Valley National Monument, California, 1990

Black Sand Pool, Yellowstone National Park, Wyoming, 1991

Goulding's Lodge, Monument Valley, Utah, 1987

Great Basin National Park, Nevada, 1987

The Courthouse, Arches National Park, Utah, I985

Bryce National Park, Utah, 1980

Zion National Park, Utah, 1988

Fishing Cone, Yellowstone National Park, Wyoming, 1990

Back Basin, Norris Geyser Basin, Yellowstone National Park, Wyoming, 1992

Grand Prismatic Spring, Yellowstone National Park, Wyoming, 1990

The Cholla Garden, Joshua Tree National Monument, California, 1986

Haleakala National Park, Maui, Hawaii, 1991

Grand Teton National Park, Wyoming, 1990

Ashton, Idaho, 1991

Lander, Wyoming, 1991

Best Western Mammoth Hot Springs, Gardiner, Montana, 1990

The Mittens, Monument Valley Navajo Tribal Park, Arizona, 1985

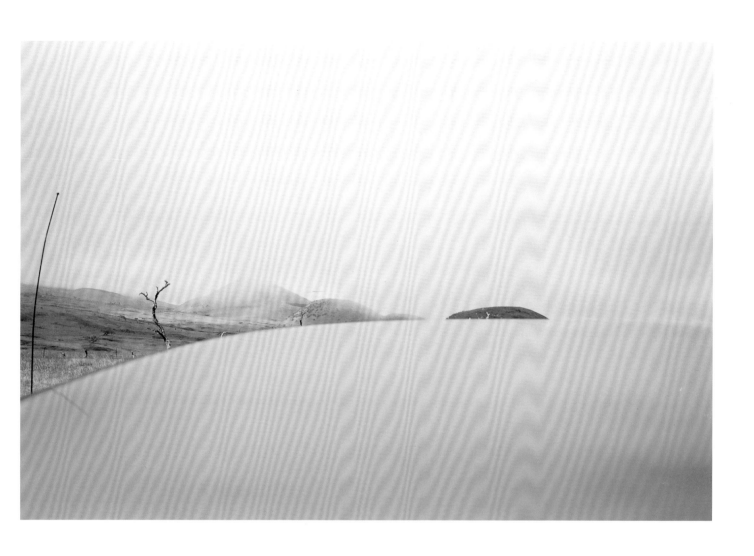

Mauna Kea, Hawaii, 1991

Hawaii Volcanoes National Park, Hawaii, 1991

Len Jenshel

Len Jenshel is today considered one of the leading photographers of the American landscape. Unlike such traditionalists as Ansel Adams, who presented the American landscape in its purity, emphasizing its transcendental and sublime aspects, Jenshel depicts the changes brought about by human presence. Sensitive to the emotional qualities of color, and finely attuned to the nuances of light, he is able to celebrate the beauty of the land while rendering the subtle ironies derived from the intrusions of tourists and commercial civilization. Often saturated in the sensuous hues of sunset, his photographs are surreal as well as haunting and mysterious. Jenshel's landscapes of this new West combine mythic qualities with an exaggerated, theatrical aspect. Overcoming the prejudices of the period against color photography and picturesque subject matter, Jenshel also radically changed his subject matter to one that was, historically, laden with cliché.

Jenshel was born in Brooklyn, New York, in 1949. He received a BFA from The Cooper Union, New York City, in 1975. Here he studied with photographers Joel Meyerowitz, Tod Papageorge, and Garry Winogrand, who were photographing mostly on the streets of New York using black-and-white film. In 1978 he received a National Endowment for the Arts grant and a New York State Council on the Arts grant, and in 1980 was awarded a Guggenheim Fellowship in photography. He has taught at Cooper Union, New York University, the School of Visual Arts, and the International Center of Photography, all in New York City.

In 1988 Jenshel received a grant from the Graham Foundation to document the American West, with an emphasis on the impact of the automobile and tourist industry on its architecture and landscape. His work has been published in *Charmed Places: Hudson River School Artists and Their Homes* (Harry N. Abrams, 1988), *The New Color Photography* (1981), *New Color—New Work* (1984), *American Independents* (1987; all Abbeville Press), and *Money Matters: A Critical Look at Bank Architecture* (McGraw Hill, 1990).

Jenshel has shown his work in numerous one-person exhibitions, notably the Art Institute of Chicago; the Carnegie Institute, Pittsburgh; and the International Center of Photography in New York. He is represented in major collections both in the United States and Europe, including the Stedelijk Museum in Amsterdam, the Boston Museum of Fine Arts, National Museum of American Art, Smithsonian Institution, the San Francisco Museum of Modern Art, and the Museum of Modern Art in New York.

The photography critic for *The New York Times* noted that Jenshel is a "member of a generation of photographers who are not afraid of the sensual, picturesque qualities of color film....[but] the message here is not solely the glories of color photography." And in 1991 *New York Magazine*, citing his most recent landscape series in which car headlights provide one light source, stated "Len Jenshel has photographed the American West better than anyone else in recent years...and the results, as always, are beautiful, quirky, and memorable."

Jenshel resides in New York City and travels extensively, photographing and lecturing on photography.

Technical Information

Jenshel makes his photographs with a 6 x 9 cm camera with a fixed wide-angle lens. He began photographing with a medium-format 6 x 9 cm Siciliano camera in 1976. Hand-made in Brooklyn, New York, it had neither mirror, light meter, timer, nor even a range-finder. In 1980 he began using another hand-made camera—the "Palm Press," which was equally crude, but had one of the sharpest lenses. Since 1985 he has used a 6 x 9 Fujica with a fixed 65mm wide-angle lens. "It really is the way I see; I see like a wide-angle lens," Jenshel states. "I rarely take verticals. As you see, every photograph in this book is horizontal." Most of the photographs in this book are 20 x 24-inch and 30 x 40-inch Type C prints. "I am amazed how well that 6 x 9 cm negative holds up in a print of that size," he says.

Jenshel prefers color negative film, and uses mostly Fujicolor, "I love the look that color negative gives me," he states. "Color transparency film could never handle the extremes of contrast that happen at dawn and dusk," the sliver of time in which he feels he does his best work. He uses natural light, and for dramatic effect he occasionally accents the landscape with a strobe or automobile headlights.